Acknowledgments

The author would like to thank the following people for sharing their expertise and enthusiasm: Sharon Brown, Beavers: Wetlands & Wildlife (website); Dr. Glynnis Hood, University of Alberta; Mike Keizer, Wood Buffalo National Park, Alberta, Canada; and John Thie, EcoInformatics International, Inc. Also a special thank-you to Skip Jeffery for his support during the creative process.

Millbrook Press
A division of Lerner Publishing Group, Inc.
241 First Avenue North
Minneapolis, MN 55401 USA

For reading levels and more information, look up this title at www.lernerbooks.com.

Main body text set in HandySans 16/22.

Library of Congress Cataloging-in-Publication Data

The Cataloging-in-Publication Data for Build, Beaver, Build! is on file at the Library of Congress.
ISBN 978-1-4677-4900-8 (lib. bdg.)
ISBN 978-1-4677-9725-2 (EB pdf)

Manufactured in the United States of America
1 – DP – 12/31/15

Build, Beaver, Build!
Life at the Longest Beaver Dam

Sandra Markle

Illustrations by
Deborah Hocking

M MILLBROOK PRESS/MINNEAPOLIS

The moon is so bright on this June
night that the pond water gleams.

A beaver kit floats near his family's lodge.

The softball-sized male is just three weeks old. His three sisters are asleep inside the lodge. But he's hungry and wants to nurse.

So he whines for his mother.

Mew-up! Mew-up!

The kit's mother is nearby, resting
on top of the family dam.

The dam, built from sticks and mud,
stretches all the way across one side
of the pond.

Another beaver family built the first part long ago. When they died, a new beaver family moved in, tending the dam and making it longer. Later still, another beaver family did the same.

Now it's the kit's family's home. But the smells of old wood and mud, mixed with fresher scents, hint at its history.

The little male kit is
swimming toward his mother
when a shadow covers him.
He looks up to see an owl
swooping down.

Diving is the kit's only chance. He does it just in time.

Then, paddling hard, he swims back to the lodge's entrance tunnel. The lodge in the pond behind his family's dam is the best place to stay safe from hungry hunters—at least while he's so small.

At eight weeks old, the male kit is football-sized and rarely nurses anymore. Now he feeds nightly at the surface of the pond.

Sometimes his parents fold up leaves for him and his sisters to eat.

More often he feeds himself.

He also gnaws on tough stuff, like cattails.

He was born with big front teeth that never stop growing. So he needs to wear them down to keep them just the right length.

When he's not eating or resting or watching out for an attack, he sneaks up on his sisters. The game soon turns to wrestling.

Pushing, rolling, and tumbling, the kits grow stronger as they play.

Usually, when the sky turns rosy with light, the beavers go inside their lodge to sleep all day. But today, the adults stay ashore a little longer, pushing up dirt piles.

The male kit mimics his mother and pushes up a mound too.

Then he follows her as she walks over
what she built, squirting out a smelly
liquid from glands at the base of her tail.

A few nights later, a male beaver arrives,
sniffs, and keeps on going. Clearly there's
a message in the scent mounds.

Stay away! This is our family dam!

Dry summer days follow dry nights.
This summer is the driest in years.

Streams shrink—then disappear. At
last, the only water around is the pond
behind the family dam. Even there the
water is so shallow deer have
to wade in to drink.

Hunters, like wolves and bears, come to drink too. Mother and father beaver watch them closely. When an otter tries to sneak up on one of the male's sisters, Mother slaps her tail on the water.

BAM! The loud noise is a surprise in the quiet night. The otter stops.

The sister dives, swims into the lodge, and stays safe.

On another evening, a Canada goose lands on the pond. It honks and honks and honks until the male kit tail-slaps the water.

Splat! His thin little tail makes more splash than noise. Still, it's enough to make the goose fly away. But not before it nips the male kit's back.

No doubt, it would be better to be bigger.

Lucky for the kit, he keeps getting bigger all summer long.

The more roots, stems, and leaves he eats, the more he grows.

And grows.
And GROWS!

By the time the days are cooler, the rains return at last. Water fills the pond again. Now the kit is big enough to practice working.

So each night, he picks up sticks the way his parents do and carries them—one by one—to the lodge or the dam to help with repairs.

But the kit never goes very far before he drops his load.

Then he rests and nibbles on the stick's tender bark.

One night, the young male follows his parents to the very end of the dam. A whisper of running water is slipping around the dam's edge, carrying away bits of sticks and mud.

The kit helps his mother and father drag sticks into the water at the end of the dam. The beavers work until the water is blocked.

And for the first time, the kit helped make the long family dam a little longer.

When the nights turn cold, the twigs
no longer taste of sap.

And the beaver parents work harder than ever,
toppling trees and gnawing off branches.
They drag these down to the pond bottom.

Slowly, they build a tangled mound outside
the lodge entrances.

It's the family's winter food supply.

The male kit and his sisters sometimes add sticks to the food pile. But just as often they steal one to snack on its tasty bark.

Winter storms arrive.
Snow blankets the land.
Ice crusts the pond.

Snug inside their
lodge, the beavers
rest and eat.

Now one year old, the young male sometimes feeds on branches his parents tug inside. But other times, he swims out to the pile of sticks and brings in food for his family.

One moonlit night, on his way to the food pile, the young male discovers a thin spot in the ice. He head-butts it until he makes a hole.

Then he crawls out. **A** breeze brings the hint of something budding. So he waddles ashore in search of fresh food. But before he goes very far, a hungry coyote charges out of the brush.

The beaver hurries across the ice, back to open water.

The coyote grabs him by the tail. But the beaver yanks free and tail-smacks the water. **BAM!**

The coyote backs up, startled. The young beaver is big enough to make a loud noise. **And** he escapes.

The nights grow warmer until, creaking and snapping, the pond's ice roof breaks into pieces. Now the air is ripe with the scent of budding aspens and leafy willows. Sometimes, after the young male eats his fill, he drags home a branch for his new baby brother and sister to nibble.

Over the winter, the beaver family has grown
another generation bigger. And the year-old male
and his sisters have much to do. They're dam builders
in training as well as babysitters.

One day, all of these skills will help the young beavers
raise families of their own.

It will be another year before
the young male leaves home.

But when he does, he'll claim a spot nearby where flowing water can be easily blocked. There, with a mate, he'll build a dam and change the world—at least part of it—into the perfect place to raise a beaver family.

A Beaver's World

Beavers are second only to humans in making major changes to their world. They cut down trees, opening an area to new kinds of plants that couldn't grow in the shade. And after nibbling the leaves and bark off branches, beavers use what's left to build a dam in flowing water. That creates a pond surrounded by marshy land. The area becomes a home for many kinds of animals besides the beavers: frogs, turtles, otters, salamanders, raccoons, waterbirds like herons and ducks, and more. In long dry periods, the beaver's pond may be the sole water source keeping animals in the area alive.

Beavers Are Amazing!

Beavers are North America's biggest kind of rodent (animals whose front teeth grow continuously). Beavers are interesting in a lot of other ways.

- Beavers' long, sharp upper and lower incisors (front teeth) have a super-hard coating containing iron. This makes them look rust orange. The backs of these teeth are softer and wear away faster than the fronts. So chewing and tooth grinding keeps the big incisors sharp.

- Beavers don't eat wood, only inner bark, leaves, stems, tubers, and roots. And to get what their bodies need out of this tough food, they have to digest it twice. The first time through their digestive systems only begins to break the food down. Then their wastes are soft, green pellets that the beavers eat. The second time through their digestive systems finish breaking down the food. Then the beavers' wastes are brown.

- Beavers are perfectly adapted for working underwater. A second set of eyelids act like goggles. And beavers' lips can be pulled together behind their big incisors. So they can bite and swim with branches in their mouths without getting a mouthful of water.

Find Out More

Arnosky, Jim. *Beaver Pond, Moose Pond*. Washington, DC: National Geographic Children's Books, 2000. Find out how the pond beaver builds to create his own special world also gives other animals a home.

Beaver Family: *National Geographic Kids*
http://video.nationalgeographic.com/ng-kids/animals-pets /beaver-kids
This mini-movie shares a year in this beaver family's life. Don't miss this chance to peek at the family at home inside their lodge.

Great Plains Nature Center: Beaver
http://www.gpnc.org/beaver.htm
Here's a chance to explore beaver facts and check out amazing photos. There's also an audio clip so you can listen to beaver noises.

Holland, Mary. *The Beaver's Busy Year*. Mount Pleasant, SC: Sylvan Dell, 2014. Enjoy a photo journey through one year of a beaver's life.

Worth a Dam: MartinezBeavers.org
http://www.martinezbeavers.org/wordpress
This site is packed with activities to make investigating beavers fun. Don't miss the "Teachers" section's activities with links to lots of games, crafts, and puzzles—all about beavers.

Author's Note

Imagine a dam made of sticks and mud so long it's big enough to be photographed by satellites from space. This dam exists in the Wood Buffalo National Park in Alberta, Canada. It's 2,788 feet (850 meters) long, and it's getting longer every year. That's because the builders are beavers, and one beaver family after another has lived there and added onto it, year after year for many years.

Scientists believe beavers have been building on this dam since the 1970s, based on evidence from aerial photos of the area. They believe the dam has lasted so many years and become so long because the land is flat, so water soaks in and doesn't flood with destructive force. Old parts of the pond may become overgrown with plant life, but the dam remains. I was intrigued to learn about that dam and to think about the beaver families, one after another, living and working on it. I wanted to learn more. What I discovered inspired me to imagine the life of a beaver kit growing up at this family dam.

LERNER
SOURCE

Expand learning beyond the printed book. Download free, complementary educational resources for this book from our website, www.lernerresource.com.

4 Glue the hat to the oak tag.

5 Draw tassle line on hat with black marker.

6 Using red marker, give Santa a round, cherry nose, two rosy cheeks, and a red bottom lip.

7 Cut a half-circle under nose.

8 Trim his hat with a strip of cotton. Use a cotton ball for the tip of his tassle. Give him a cotton beard and a twirly mustache. Give him two cotton eyebrows.

9 Glue everything in place.

10 Stick a loose-leaf reinforcement behind each ear around the holes.

11 Tie two pieces of yarn or string through the holes.

CHRISTMAS BALLS

Here's what you need:

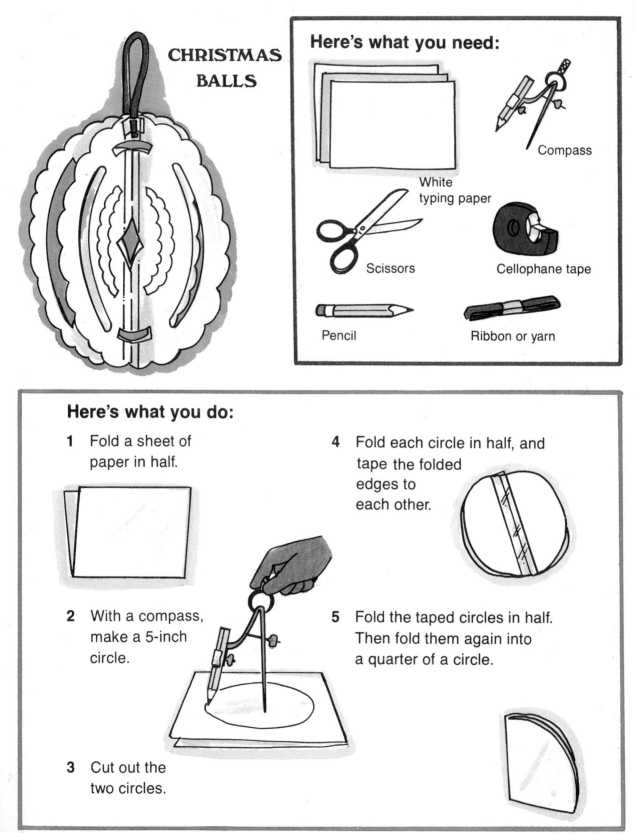

White typing paper

Compass

Scissors

Cellophane tape

Pencil

Ribbon or yarn

Here's what you do:

1 Fold a sheet of paper in half.

2 With a compass, make a 5-inch circle.

3 Cut out the two circles.

4 Fold each circle in half, and tape the folded edges to each other.

5 Fold the taped circles in half. Then fold them again into a quarter of a circle.

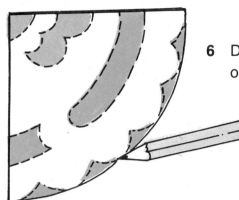

6 Draw a design on the folded circle. Copy this one, or make one of your own.

7 With your scissors, carefully cut out the design.

8 Take an 8-inch piece of ribbon or yarn, and place a strip of cellophane tape at each end.

9 Open the folded circles to make two complete circles. Tape the ribbon to the circles to form a loop for hanging the ornament. Hang it from a window shade. Or hang it from a lamp. Or hang it from a gift-wrapped box to make an extra pretty package.

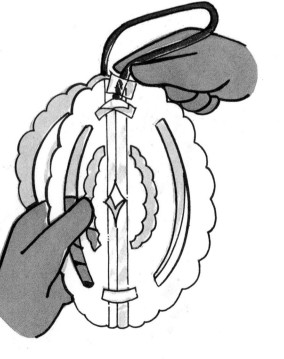

Here's what you need:

White typing paper

Compass

Scissors

Pencil

Glue

SNOWFLAKES

Here's what you do:

1 With a compass, draw the biggest circle you can on a sheet of typing paper.

2 Cut out the circle, and fold it in half.

3 Fold the half into thirds. Make sharp creases along the folds.